Looking at Renaissance Paintings and Other Poems

Looking at Renaissance Paintings and Other Poems

June 11, 2011

For Terry, Warm regards

Caroline Morgan Di Giovanni

Caroline Morgan Di Giovanni

QUATTRO BOOKS

Cover art: Detail of *The Annunciation* (1430-1432) by Fra Angelico, Museo del Prado
Cover design: Diane Mascherin

Library and Archives Canada Cataloguing in Publication

DiGiovanni, Caroline Morgan,
Looking at Renaissance paintings and other poems / Caroline Morgan DiGiovanni.

Poems.
ISBN 978-0-9782806-8-0

I. Title.
PS8607.I44L66 2008 C811'.6 C2008-905990-5

Published by
Quattro Books
P.O. Box 53031
Royal Orchard Postal Station
10 Royal Orchard Blvd.
Thornhill, ON L3T 3C0
www.quattrobooks.ca

Printed in Canada

This is dedicated
to the ones I love

Contents

Looking at Renaissance Paintings

Portraits and Miniatures

Looking at Renaissance Paintings

Looking at Renaissance Paintings

I

It was an age of faith and universal
affiliation with the course of nature.
God was the Almighty.
His Son died to save us,
the Holy Spirit wrapped wide wings around.

Stars circled their celestial rounds as surely
as the seasons followed after one another.
Righteous rulers ruled by grace, unless
another one more powerful prevailed.
Duty was done. Courtesy expected.
The lives of men and women
strictly delineated.

Inside this world, on the
boot-shaped peninsula, under a
glorious sun, perfect conditions
for colour, light, abundance,
into the flourishing courtyards
of the great and grand
there came the artists,
ready to do work.

They painted walls of chapels and churches
with Genesis or Matthew, or the lives of saints,
and in the corner, modestly apart,
the patron and his consort, exquisitely gowned.
The artists had a kinship with each other,
sometimes apprenticeship, or workshop labour.
So many artists, so rich an endowment,
their world portrayed in pigment, stone, and statue.

Today we marvel at their gifts of beauty.
One wonders even more,
and is it gone from us?
their gift of faith.

II

The artists of the age of space
imagine anything
one drop of water
expounded into elements
frozen on the planet Mars
carries the creative heartbeat.

The exploration into art
resembles travel into space
tchnology required
science studied
workshop apprenticeship
the jealous measure each of other.

The gift of possibilities
the challenge of selection
the isolation and the doubt
draped like a cloak across the back
the moment on the brink of the void
then music, colour, light, and form.

Time re-invented
beautiful dynamo
art as the soul of creation.

The Artist Contemplates the Void

Inspired by the fresco cycle in San Gimignano

First Panel: Creation of the Heavens

Oh God how do I begin
to show the way the world began?
I lie on my back at midnight
look up at the stars
imagine
the most perfect void –
A circle? dark? light? silence?
Before the wind, what did the wind whisper?

Tomorrow I must start but where,
and how do I begin to paint
what no one has ever seen
in all the ages before me?

I am small beside the universe.

The plaster is ready
I pick up my brush
for the first stroke
"In the beginning was the Word."

Second Panel: Garden of Eden

God is walking in the garden.
Unknowable Yahweh
a burning bush won't do.
The Roman statue in the courtyard
won't do.

Man is made in the image of God
and so reversed,
God must look like
Geraldo, who sells me wine
a beautiful face,
but so young
Ennio, the man of learning,
wisdom has a human visage
Celestino, the shoemaker's son,
still innocent of carnal knowledge
Bartolomeo the Idiot,
unable to sin.

God in the Garden of Eden
my image to create.

Michelangelo in the Sistine Chapel

I am the artist Michelangelo.
Here I am perched on a scaffold
up against the ceiling,
as close as I can get
to Paradise.

There are some days I curse
the proud priest who put me here,
some days I bless him
for the grace to paint
the holy scenes of God
creating everything we know.

Too large a task!
My hands quake,
my back aches,
I swoon from discomfort
and in ecstasy.

What am I but a man astonished
by an awesome power
coursing through me.
I can hardly understand it.
I only know that I am given to create
another world, an unchanging scene
made of the human bodies that I see
forming the perfect vision in my mind.

I cannot stop. I will not stop
to rest. There is no rest.
I am possessed.

Adam stands before me in the garden.
God makes him a consort, Lady Eve,
flesh of his flesh.
How beautiful their bodies are,
innocent in the joy of life.
God's hand extended in creation
a greater monument this, than any cathedral.

Tondo

What are they doing there
that line of naked men
behind the Holy Family
in the museum?

What the hell?
You come all the way from
New Jersey or wherever
to see the art before lunch
and it hits you,
this line of beach boys
behind the Madonna and Joseph
and the Baby Jesus.

I'm outside under the hot sun
waiting for the wife to quit
shopping, and I'm still thinking
God, what are they doing
in that famous picture –
the line of perfectly naked men
behind the Holy Family?

Hell's Mouth

The exit of the church at San Gimignano
makes the faithful congregation
walk through hell.
Imagine
every Sunday mothers
guiding their scrubbed and wiggling offspring
under the glare
of dusky devils swinging pointed tails
grinning their horrible grins
dismembering
the fleshy sinners, women especially,
stretched and violated
in pornographic poses.

Seen every Sunday
what did this do but
titillate the little boys and make
the girls weirdly uncomfortable.

No questions asked were answered.
"Just believe
that if you're bad
the devil takes you in
and you will join the wraiths
strung on the ceiling."

On the other side of the portal,
calm and clean,
the saints
roll their eyes up to heavenly clouds,
sing alleluia and enjoy
unending boredom bordering on bliss.

Given the choice
the ten year old will pick
the raucous noise and ranting,
the grinding and the panting.

Triptych

I. My Passion Movie

Me, I would put Jesus
in a concentration camp.
He would speak with an accent,
having come in from the countryside
to work in Berlin.

The characters around him,
looking gaunt,
despair of saving themselves.
A fella named Job
sits all day in the dust,
his mind fixed on perplexities.

But Jesus, in my movie,
goes about doing his job of work.
He carries the stones for the wall,
he is clever with wood
so the guards get him to make chairs.

He makes a set of nine chairs,
beautiful chairs.
The judges sit in the chairs
facing a long looking glass
when they pronounce the final
order.

II. Memling Madonna

There is in the
Philadelphia Museum
a Memling Madonna
fourteen or fifteen, pure.

A portrait of her face
the light translucent
brown hair unadorned
by elaborate Renaissance jewels.
Her eyes are the jewels,
simple, in wonder.

The search for beauty
a grand ideal
the model merely
a sweet young girl.

No background, no landscape
no embroidered collar
no angel announcing anything
no bird in the window.

A young girl now aware
of her precious gift and
her suddenly awesome
power.

III. Let's Think about Joseph

Such a fine old man
patient and loving
grey beard and all
good at making things
good at taking care
listening and dreaming
at opportune moments.

How is it, Joseph,
you believed the angel?
Wishful thinking after all,
or worth the lovely prize
and all her baggage?

Now you appear as background
logistical support
manager of the whole thing,
but back then
when it happened

You had questions,
didn't you?

Fratello Francesco

The Basilica in Assisi

While I am sitting here waiting
for Death to arrive at my door
I think about you, my Brother,
you who awoke from your sleep
fresh and new. Innocent.
Ready to talk to the birds.
You, my Fratello Francesco
going naked into the woods in winter.

Giotto saw you a hundred years later.
You were timeless by then.
He saw you face to face –
he gave over his brushes and colours
to be guided by your hand
for you were of Assisi
and on those walls
you knew the stories to tell
to shake the souls of the pilgrims.

Looking at poppies in the fields in May
or the sunflowers turning their heads
under the Umbrian sun
every tourist who walks there
will meet you
coming at them, barefoot
Fratello Francesco sanctissimus.

The Catherine Story

St. Catherine of Siena,
a mad woman,
rose on her toes in ecstasy
and floated up the stairs.

She never ate, preferring
to waste her earthly body
anorexia nervosa
including long walks in the rain.

Today some supermodels
waste away like that,
and schizophrenia captures
the mind in awkward ways.

But are these visions sacred?
Who can tell? Elias is nowhere
to be seen, and no angels
come to force-feed Catherine.

Her mission was smart politics,
the papal mess required
jostling and shoving, conniving
strategic backroom deals.

O, Catherine, did they use you
or did you put them to use
to reach your lofty end? Holiness
or hallucination: saints or cynics?

Faith is a gift
that turns on all the lights.
Shadows disappear when you believe –
then there's no holding back.

Easter Duty

Delicate, blooming, tender, yellow, pink,
blue, violet, white, and a whole
vocabulary of bright, varied green
rises from the earth like hope.
By what miracle does this emerge
from the grey grief of winter?

The word is love –
but which of us can say it
without hypocrisy?
The cock crows thrice
the first stone is thrown
the serpent slides away, gloating.

Only a child's eyes can see
the robin's nest with wonder.
Now is the time to search for open water,
the broken ice gone,
reflecting the intense blue sky
and our own sorry face, looking down.

Annunciations Everywhere

Annunciations everywhere.
Angels of all sorts,
dressed in fine robes
cinctured, sandaled,
wings and hair arranged
for the great visitation.
A final rehearsal, bow
to the Great Light
then off through the stars
to the blue jewel hanging
at the edge of that piece of sky,

bearing a message to ignite
a revolution like no other.

The young Maria, unaware,
goes about her dutiful day
rising early,
dressing and combing
cleaning the little room,
a fresh bunch of flowers
(always white lilies).
She opens the window, the light
streams in wonderfully,
the book illuminated –

then a sudden rustle of wings
an apparition and a voice
to be reckoned with.

Fiat voluntas tuas
My soul doth magnify the Lord.

Angels: Deconstructed

If angels came today to a convention
where
would they hang their wings?
Would they have wings at all?
Or would they simply float
like astronauts, turning
upsidedown, weightless?

And if in fact there actually are
such entities called angels
as in ages past
would we still see them wearing
long white robes and,
in the case of Michael,
equipped with a broadsword?

What if these creations
exist only in cyberspace
as light beams, ethereal,
time=energy: not even atoms
generated for the analytic eyes
of our accelerated age?

So do we even need angels
today when we have so many
tumultuous and agitating
couriers of every kind?

Except the messengers who bring
comfort in the desert,
miracles,
and warnings.

Il mio amico Shakespeare

What if our William Shakespeare stowed away
or took a job as deckhand on a ship
bound for Venezia and ports unknown?
He might have been storm-toss'd and felt the thrill
of rescue from a wide, deserted strand,
and once in Venice he would see the crowds
of merchants, fakirs, all the hoi polloi
of east and west and north and south –
what stories told to feed his poetry!

The romance of his soul, the fire of passions,
his sympathetic eye, attuned to beauty,
would comprehend the fruit and bloom of nature,
and riches made by craftsmen out of gold,
the jewels and silk, the pearl upon the ear
of the exquisite Ethiop, the sun
at noonday on the glittering piazza.

Shakespeare in Italy, a dream of translocation.
How did he come to taste and feel and see
and hear the very music of the place?
Truly the mystery and gift of genius.
When other sailors headed out to seek
the brave new world, young William packed
his travels in his head, and took his pen
and wrote a wide dramatic world instead.

Sonnet about Silence

I live in silence. No one wants to hear
my voice in lamentation all the time.
It's boring for the audience to bear
the burden of depression. What a crime
to work at nothing better than a rhyme
made out of nothing, no specific thing
to do or say except to pass the time.
I wait all day just for the phone to ring –
"Hello, hello, old friend, how good to know
that we are still alive, as of today.
The world is going swimmingly" or so
it seems appropriate for me to say.
No depth, no truth, no insight to disclose
a day like all the others, heaven knows.

The Constant Pain of Love

The moving grey sky opens up the day.
Birds sing as usual. The time goes by.
I sit and write but don't know what to say.
Nothing comes easy. Words appear to lie.

And then out of the blue, unbidden, comes
the anxious doubt, the constant pain of love,
like Macbeth's witches pricking in their thumbs.
If I could change the world I would change love –

restore it like the grace of spring, to see
the bright surprising blossoms on a tree,
or hot with summer's lusty, luscious days
when we danced joyfully in ancient ways –
the double helix winding or some such
conveyance back to the first glance, first touch.

Farewell Sonnet

The day has finally come when we should part,
when we should say good-bye and there it ends.
You were not one to share with me your heart,
and I'm not one who wants to be "just friends."

And there it is. We both are young and so
there's lots of time to find somebody new.
Like other pairs before us, we can go
along our separate ways and still be true

to the sweet youth we shared in summer days.
Your laugh will always be the archetype
of joyful moments, silly fun, and ways
we shared the sweetness when the fruit was ripe.

Go on now. You're not serious, I see.
That is the difference for you and me.

Audition

The once-aspiring dancer danced alone
for hours in the mystery of sound
and muscle memory and discipline
and body language codified, perfected.

The dancer wanted everything to move
in harmony and rhythm, strength and grace,
the patterns deep embedded in the bone
practiced to keep the balance, lift and leap.

The dancer always wanted to be fine,
come to the stage in costume, curtain rising
the audience attentive, hushed, enchanted
magic unfolding in the turns and gestures.

It wasn't quite enough. Perhaps a fall,
an awkward dissonance. Dancer, dream on.

Passion

I have in my possession
an antique stiletto
bejeweled and elegant
a gift from Italy
land of passion and beauty.

This precision instrument
the story goes
belonged to a Contessa
renowned for the flash of her temper
and her cunning green eyes.

I touch the dangerous point
and ask myself
whose heart
is this intended for,
and why am I holding it now?

Portraits and Miniatures

Clouds

Poems can be like clouds
like simple clouds, little clouds
visible from the ground below
giving the curious farmer
a reason to look up and wonder
"Does this cloud carry something
I need to know about?
Is there a burden of meaning
within the fleecy edges?"

Once in a while even a poem
can explode into lightning
and thunder. Ask Dante.
Ask William.
Ask Carl.

Walking with Anne in the Boboli Gardens

We are in Firenze.
The years have been kind
to our friendship.
Here we are walking together
in the Boboli Gardens.

Statues from ages past
silent in their niches
the green grass burns hot
pine trees rustle
a small breeze resonates
across the lake of dreams.

Friends from the seaside
two teenage girls silly
and sharing stories together,
cold swims in the salt water bay
dreaming of the days to come
when the grand life would begin.

Today in the Boboli Gardens
"women of a certain age"
we tell stories of
the worlds we have known,
the fountains, box hedges, and roses
blown, fragrance lingering,
joy to share.

In a Roman Market

Today I am a Roman *donna di casa.*
I walk through the market stalls
searching for the freshest fish,
the peach without blemish.

This corner looks good –
I'll wait behind the anxious *signora*
planning for guests this evening,
everything must be perfect!
"Don't try to give me those lemons,
they look as old as the *colosseo*."

Basilica, whole leaves, bright green.
Pesce spada big as a child,
eyes open and sword on display –
I hope he put up a good fight.

This is the way Rome continues
from age to age.
In the life of the city,
the housewives run the engine
with their daily march to the market,
the back and forth/vendor to buyer
farmer and fisherman/
cook and connoisseur.

All the men in tailored suits
who believe they rule the country
would fall down, exhausted,
without the beating
of this great heart.

The Italian Parenting Handbook

Cover them with kisses
when they're young.

Mothers and fathers both
hugs and kisses in abundance
on the street and
in the park, and
at the breakfast table.

Everywhere – cover the babies
and children with your *baci,*
bacetti, and hugs, and
loving little words, and
sweetini names.

When they are naughty
(and everyone sometimes is)
let them know it right away –
the closest parent or *zia* or
nonno or person at the next table
must let the naughty one know
that is a no-no.

Then

Cover the babies and children
with kisses and hugs.

They are loved,
so loved and cherished
these children of Italy
they will be a gift
to the world.

Exactly Alberto

Based on a photograph taken in the mountains

Here is Alberto standing
in the field of a mountain meadow
in Abruzzo, Italy.

Behind him the sky
forms a tiny corner
of the picture.

Mountains are everything.
Alberto's village rests
in the palm of the Maiella.

There he was nurtured with iron milk,
cradled in the arms of integrity,
fed on the food of truth and
given the courage to speak it.

From this rock
Alberto watched
the eagles fly
                    the eagles fly
                                        away.

Mare

The green waves of the sea
extending outward,
carry us away.

Oh my beloved,
here with you
we reconstruct the first amphibian's landing,
   fish-fins turned to feet
   eagerly beating gills trans-
   mogrify into air sacs, tissues
   lungs and heart, pumping
A miracle!

And still the sea
could claim us back
in an instant, jealous
of our freedom to walk about.

The green and dark blue ocean,
the laughing waves of the sea.

Lucy, Dancing

She dances
under the high bright moon
alone
the music pulses
through her.

She sparkles and shines
and as she moves
she holds back
time.

Island rhythm
the palm trees waving
stars in the blue black sky.

The warm breeze
sweeps clouds away
a celestial aura surrounds her

And the spectators
clap their hands
all for Lucy,

dancing.

Lunar Eclipse

Mothers and daughters
come and watch
the shadow of the earth
creeping incrementally
to cover up the moon.

The rhythms of the oceans
all depend
upon the moon
and Sister Moon lights sidewalks
for the waitress going home.

"Mooon" says baby
breast milk moon
life giving
while Dante Alighieri
swoons in ecstasy
approaching Paradise.

Mothers and daughters
know why there is silence
at the eclipse
of the perfect moon.

In the Royal Botanical Gardens

Burlington, Ontario

Slight sliver of moon
soft sound of jazz
mist from the
          cascading
                    fountains
fragrant evening air
          summer blooming gardens
                    all around

Take this evening
wrapped up in wonder
take this evening
home in your pocket
for that time in November
when all the trees
are bare.

My Aunt Annie's Recipe for Fudge

My Aunt Annie had very long black hair
even in old age, not a wisp of white.
Early morning, she would comb it down
in the mud room, before the house awakened.
I would watch her. That is how I knew
the secret of those crafty wire hairpins
tucking each circlet perfectly in place.

Aunt Annie understood the mystery of keeping house.
All the eight others, out to work or wed
but she stayed home to do whatever was needed
to keep up: cooking, cleaning, sewing
curtains, a winter coat, a wedding dress.

Summer in the big house at the beach
my Aunt Annie was the spirit of the place.
The lobster pot, the big round table, full,
jolly with food and folks, nobody left out.
Evenings, rocking on the high, wide porch
her comfy lap was the best place to nestle
watching the splendid sunset over the bay,
me the only girl child in a passel of boys.

Aunt Annie liked her martini before dinner.
She liked to laugh at a good joke, tell a story,
pick her horses, make a list, and pay her two dollars
when the uncles went off to the racetrack.
At night she said her rosary on wooden beads,
a gift for her from Rome, brought back by

her nephew who became a priest.
With the house full she would sleep her few hours
on the pull-out bed in the back bedroom.

My Aunt Annie taught me how to make
the most delicious fudge in the whole world.
The recipe included a piece of butter
the size of a walnut.

Joseph on the Rooftop

For Msgr. J. Joseph Ryan

Like some ancient prophet
there was Joseph
standing on the rooftop at night
surrounded by flames.

"How did this happen?" he says
to himself as
the fire engines roar.
"Hey, I was in my sickbed
ten minutes ago."

God works in mysterious
waves. The seeing eye
discerns beneath the smoke
and other confusion
a test of strength.

"You will come to me Joseph
not yet but soon.
Rise up and walk.
Your faith has saved you."

Stronger than the super-pumper
stronger than the hook-and-ladder
stronger than the frail old man
in hospital pyjamas.

Al Purdy Sits in Queen's Park

The poet sits down on a slab of rock
some part of the Canadian Shield
could be yesterday or
whenever he first began dreaming.
This poet is a man of words
plain words, but always taken
with care from the word bag
to fit around the ideas he had.
Ideas as big as the Prairies or
Niagara Falls, or the Galapagos Islands, or
they might travel backwards in time
to ancient days, before first human footprints.

Al Purdy, phenomenal Al
sits down now in Queen's Park,
a stone's throw from the dinosaurs
embedded in the walls of the ROM.
At the south end of the park stands
the Pink Palace where the MPPs
spend Question Period making accusations
(and by the by occasionally making laws).
Al must chuckle at their fearsome bluster.
He cocks his head and looks
towards St. Michael's College
where Marshall McLuhan taught poetry
for years between his musings on
the Global Village.

Just north there, on the curve
of Queen's Park Crescent,
he sees Victoria College where that other
giant professor Northrop Frye held sway.
"The truth shall make you free"
the doorway declares, and that is where
young Peggy Atwood first learned how to write.

The image of Al Purdy takes his place
right in the centre,
listening, conjuring words, thinking in lines
as poets always do,
their words living beyond them,
statue or no.

Somersaulting Man: "As I Think of Myself"

Stone carving by John Kavik, 1964. Art Gallery of Ontario

Tumbling backwards
face
full of joy

free to fly
nearly
earthbound, but

free
spirit free
free to tumble over

flexible, but
balanced
on only
two hands

The centre holds
eyes open
energetic

suddenly
arrested

As others think of you
As I think of
my
self.

Pathetique

There she is
and there she is again
a woman of such potential
sitting on a park bench
in the sun.
And if you ask
"What do you do all day?"
the answer comes back plain –
"When I am wandering
I just write letters."
And some of them are mailed away
and some remain
in the air
...of such potential
...sitting in the sun.

What It Is To Be a Shadow

The wife
the big sister
the first one on stage

Martha to Mary
editor not author
"Special thanks to…"

The end of the credits
scrolling as the audience
leaves the theatre

What it is
not to draw conclusions
to enable
not to act

Like waxed paper
for safekeeping
like quill pens
a good sharp tip
but never the
real words.

Luminous Snail

This is the life of
the luminous snail

Silent and occupied
moving slowly, slowly

The path may be
uncomfortable

But it leads out
through the gateway.

Shoo Pigeons

Shoo pigeons – away from here
this is no place
for you to nest

Go take those twigs and threads
away and find
a safer haven
somewhere else

We are both of species caught
between town and country
we both like to stroll
down the centre
of Main Street or
the Piazza San Marco

But oh no – you have to go
you've got the gift
of wings to fly
I only hold title
to this balcony.

Old House

This is the house of
late nights, sleepless nights.

All the dark corners
creak and groan, creak and
cause chaos.

Roots go down deep,
branches tower over.
The pruning has been neglected.

Other priorities prevail,
like talking about cruelty
and cruelty itself.

Swimming Pool

We are the women of grace.
A morning light
comes to us, and
we shine like the water
that holds us.

Before this day all our days
were busy with exigencies.

Our dutiful days
now open
into freedom.

Enjoy the sunlight!
  blue sky/water/time

Enjoy the moment
  wise to the way of it.

The Wisteria of Mississippi

For Aunt Betty

How I would like to travel south
at the time of the Mississippi spring,
to see the wisteria growing
purple and lush
blooming to life again
after a dreary winter.

I've never been to Chatawa
but they tell me
the sky above can
take your breath
away.

And the grand congregation of blossoms
every color in the catalogue
meant to do nothing but
gladden the heart!

I've never seen the Pearly Gates
but they tell me
the wisteria of a Mississippi spring
may be just as beautiful
as heaven.

Sunday Morning News

A man is running towards the camera,
his arm extended.

A man runs towards the camera,
mouth agape, eyes gleaming wildly,
his arm extended in a frantic gesture.

The camera is a keyhole.
The man enters my apartment through the keyhole.
He follows me down the hallway, and
onto the elevator.

The man runs beside me in the park.
His words incoherent, at least to my ears,
he stays close behind me in the subway tunnel.

Now I am frightened. His arm gestures frantically.
I cannot understand his words.
He runs behind me in my dreams at night.

The camera is the keyhole.
The man and all his agony
entered my home
through the keyhole.

Louisiana Wild

September 2, 2005

This is the day
we never thought would come.
The sky swept in, the rain
poured down like Noah's deluge,
the flood submerged the town.
My brother is dead. My sister
washed away.
I lost my baby,
snatched out of my arms
by god or the devil,
I can't say which one.
I want to die myself
everything gone.
No home to go home to,
the streets alive with fire,
danger at every turn,
gunfire and snakes,
destruction, anger, rape,
my misery is endless –
I am New Orleans
The Queen of the Mississippi
The Crescent City.
My rhythm, unforgettable, intense
dangerous as a Mardi Gras whore
respectable as an ante bellum mansion.

My heart is broken now
worse than warfare
broken by my own.

Honouring Jordan

For Jordan Manners, 2007

This is a poem to honour Jordan
for I am his mother
and my son is dead.
It doesn't matter to me that
he is black and I am white.
It doesn't matter to me that
he has a mother,
bowing down in grief.

Jordan is the son of every mother
living in this city.
Every boy who goes outside
to play with friends
to run and laugh and learn
should grow into a man.
And every mother has the right
to watch that boy become
a leader, a worker, a husband, a
person with dreams and ambition...

Jordan is my son.
He is every mother's son.
His passing is the unspeakable.
His mother's anguish cuts into my soul.

Chartreuse Hair

So here's the thing
my stepdad, like,
he hates me but
he loves my mom
so after too much shouting
once, i'm off the couch and
out the door.

My friend, like this girl sophie
she does hair. i went to her place
and i said like do it purple
you know, or maybe green
something wild
like screaming.

(already I have this ring, like,
in my nose but it's not enough
this time anyway)

Chartreuse, says sophie
that's what you want
elegant and mysterious
you have to keep your dignity
intact.

Sunset at Lake Ariel

October, 2005

I Through the door of many days
I enter.
The wise women at the threshold
hold open the portal
with memories,
    dreams, and
        desires…
Am I the key
    or the mirror?

II One says:
  My childhood is here again.
  The long lane winds through the willows.
  My brothers walk beside me,
    going to school at a
    hurry-up pace.
  We spy a deer
    in the shadows.

III The other finds an aid to memory
  in the view of the lake in October –
  there were spectacular sunsets
  colors spilled across the horizon
  liquid iridescence on the ocean.
  We could see the whole of it
  summer evenings,
  on the veranda.

IV And all the sorrows of the past
and all the young men gone to war
and all the love that did not last
these I remember,
in my bed at night.
The darkness hides them, and
darkness brings them back.

I long for the sky of morning.

V For a woman who has done
nothing all her life but serve
others, the experience of having
time on her hands is very hard
to take. What to do. It is a puzzle
needs to be assembled. Some of
the pieces are jagged, like the fire
in the house, or the flood waters.

VI Three places are set at the table
one for Katherine
one for Mary
one for Caroline.

The grace of mealtime descends.
The wine is poured
ancient custom
Nature's boon.
Another meal begins.

Here present there are many names
voices, faces, laughs and gestures.
The talk circles the globe:

Toronto, Philadelphia, New Orleans, Boston
Rome, Siena, Florence, Pescara
Washington, New York, San Diego, Alexandria
Largo, Houston, Santa Cruz, Pascagoula

Japan, Kenya, China, England
France, Germany, Netherlands, Italy
Mexico, Portugal, Dominican Republic
Canada, Vietnam, Hong Kong, Australia

How in a lifetime
of humble routine
the world comes round to us –
how we embrace the world.

VII Each day a gift
the brilliant light on trees
yellow,
gold,
scarlet
mirrored on the surface
of quiet lake water.

A peaceful rendering
of time and day and season.
Time passing,
leaves fall on the surface,

the current of the deep
barely
        perceptible.

VIII My back aches now.
For ninety years
I've stood upright.
    Today –
today I must admit
my bones are weary.

They curve in on each other.

Nine decades is a long time
to stand steady and hold fast.

Time Poem

Let's talk about time
together, you and I
how long it takes
to comprehend

The morning
lasts forever when
the door shuts behind you

A day is a year
light years
the distance between us

Stardust and other planets
intervene

How long is it I miss you
beyond measure.

Faithful

Safe in your arms
this is not sentimental
long years together
match us skin to skin.

We are different together
Always the mysterious other
wisdom lives in that.

The day to day
coffee and toast
phone messages
locating the postage stamps
none of it important when

I see you in the night
your glasses off
and your tired face
resting.

Author's Notes

The **Duomo of San Gimignano** is decorated with frescos depicting scenes from the Old Testament on one side, painted by Bartolo di Fredi, and scenes from the life of Christ on the other side, painted by Barna di Siena. The entrance paintings with scenes of hell and heaven were painted by Benozzo Gozzoli and Taddeo di Bartolo. Such large commissions were completed with the assistance of workers who applied the plaster, and apprentices from the artists' workshops, who mixed colours and filled in backgrounds.

In 1508 **Michelangelo Buonarroti** was commissioned by Pope Julius II to decorate the ceiling of the Sistine Chapel with scenes from the Book of Genesis. Although he much preferred to work as a sculptor, he learned the fresco technique for this magnificent undertaking. He completed the ceiling in October, 1512. Later, from 1535 to 1541, he painted The Last Judgment on the wall above the main altar, for Pope Paul III.

Tondo (rotondo) refers to a painting on a round canvas and in a round frame. Wealthy families commissioned such paintings to decorate their villas. The Holy Family by Michelangelo hangs in the Uffizi Museum in Florence.

The story of the **Annunciation** describes the visit of an angel to the young Virgin Mary, telling her that she was chosen by God to be the mother of the Messiah. This subject appears in every cycle of the life of Christ and the life of Mary, decorating churches and altarpieces throughout the Renaissance period. There are fine examples by Fra Angelico, Leonardo Da Vinci, and Sandro Botticelli, among the many representations of this scene.

The **Basilica of St. Francis in Assisi** was constructed in the 13th century as the tomb for the body of St. Francis and his first followers, and to serve as a monastery for the friars in the Franciscan order. Artists from all over Italy came to decorate the walls and altars. Scenes from the life of St. Francis fill the walls of the main basilica, painted by the great Florentine artist Giotto di Bondone.

Acknowledgements

Having waited until midlife to gather my poems together into a book, I have a very long list of people to thank for inspiration. There is no place to begin, nor can I be selective. I want to thank them all: family, friends, teachers, colleagues, and a whole host of creative artists whose work I deeply admire. Without them, not a line would have been written.

On the practical side, bringing out a book requires patience and persuasion, helpful advice, criticism, compliments, enthusiasm, and editing. For all of these, I am happy to acknowledge and thank the following: the four principals of Quattro Books, in particular my editor, Allan Briesmaster; the wide circle of Italian Canadian writers I've gotten to know, especially Caterina Edwards, Gianna Patriarca, Darlene Madott, and Pier Giorgio Di Cicco; my daughters Franca and Annamaria Di Giovanni; my son Carlo and his wife Laura Foster Di Giovanni; and of course more than anyone else my husband Alberto Di Giovanni who introduced me to Italy and to the joy of our enduring love and marriage.